Guerrilla Apologetics

for
Catholics

by Paul E. Nowak

ISBN 0-9772234-0-X

Special thanks to my friends and fellow homeschoolers. While you may not have shared my beliefs, you strengthened my faith and inspired Guerrilla Apologetics.

Table of Contents

Introduction

Apologetics, the defense of one's faith, is not enjoyed by everyone. None the less, we have all been called to participate in interfaith dialog – especially those of us who encounter people of other faiths on a daily basis at work, at school, or in public places. In such cases, our duty to engage in interfaith dialog is unavoidable.

If you're reading this book, odds are you're Catholic and have been asked on at least one occasion about your beliefs. Some of you have been asked many times, even daily, or weekly, or whenever you see that friend, co-worker, neighbor or family member who just cannot seem to understand why and how you can be a Catholic. Sometimes the questions come at inopportune times, such as in the workplace where religious discussion is generally taboo. At these times it is nearly impossible to give a proper in-depth response, much less have the resources at your fingertips!

Some of you have even experienced a pressured conversation from non-Catholic Christians regarding your beliefs. During these hard-sell evangelism sessions it can be difficult to keep your cool, and even more so to have ready answers to a torrent of questions and a rapid-fire volley of Bible verses.

This book was written to aid you in these situations, by using a unique approach to Catholic apologetics. In the previous examples and almost any other book on apologetics, it is assumed that the Catholic will only be providing answers to questions from challengers; in other words, we Catholics typically take a defensive position.

While playing defense is perfectly fine, it is certainly not the most effective technique. It relies too heavily on knowing all the answers to the nearly infinite number of questions that might be posed by individuals from any of the splintered parts of the Church – which is impossible, not to mention time-consuming just to attempt. Volumes have been written with answers to these questions, and it would be foolish to try to commit them to memory.

In addition, it is never a good strategy in any competition (for such discussions are, in the spirit of good debate, competitions) to wear your opponent out by standing on the defensive. Boxers do not stand and block until their opponent collapses, chess players must make offensive moves during the game, and competitive sports cannot generally be won without scoring a few points during the struggle. Likewise, it is a very difficult (not to mention long) process to convince someone that the Catholic Church is the true Church of Christ by waiting until you have convincingly answered all of his or her objections.

Therefore, this book proposes a new strategy – taking the offensive. In terms of apologetics, this means taking the initiative and asking questions, instead of just answering them. Rather than memorizing responses for countless questions, keep in mind a handful of questions for others that will make them reflect on their own beliefs. After all, it stands to reason that if we are standing on the rock foundation of the True Church, there must be cracks in the theology of those who challenge it.

In other words, if a Protestant asks why you are Catholic, go ahead and ask them why they are not! There are many aspects of the Christian life, even Scripture, that point to Catholicism, and many Protestants are not aware of them.

This method produces three noticeable benefits: First, the challenger is usually surprised when confronted with a question, idea, or Bible verse they are not familiar with. It is an unfortunate truth that there are churches that train their members in the assault on Catholics, but once off the track of their rote recitation of verses, they get lost and lose momentum. Second, asking questions is more charitable and is better received than getting defensive. Thirdly, it makes the discussion into a conversation, instead of an inquisition, when both parties take turns questioning and being questioned.

Due to the fact the method is irregular for apologetics, is offensive (as opposed to defensive) in nature, and has a more strategic element to it, I refer to it as "Guerrilla Apologetics." While it was named with the revolutionary "Guerrilla Marketing" business strategy in mind, the technique can also be similar to hit-and-fade tactics used in guerrilla warfare – especially when you are approached in the workplace or other situations where you must make a point clearly and quickly, using questions that make the greatest impact in only a few moments.

However, it is very important that while you take the offensive with your arguments, that you yourself do not take on a manner that is offensive to others. While this point is discussed further in the first chapter, it is so important I will mention it here as well – your actions, including your tone, body language, and mannerisms will speak much louder than your words, and shouting the other person down or insulting their beliefs is counter-productive, discouraging, and unfit behavior for a follower of Christ.

On a final note, this book is written for Catholics. It assumes that you already know and believe the basics of Church teaching. Give copies to your Catholic friends, relatives, youth groups, teachers, and priests, but refrain from giving it to Protestant friends – as it is intended for Catholics, it is not written for someone who does not believe as we do. Rather, use the book to enter into an engaged conversation, and draw from your own belief to show that the Catholic Church is not only defensible, but Christ's true Church.

Keep the Faith,

Paul Nowak

Guerrilla Apologetics 101

Before going into the details of using Guerrilla Apologetics, it is important that the goal is made clear. The purpose of using Guerrilla Apologetics is to turn the discussion into a conversation with give-and-take on both sides, and to plant seeds for God to develop in the other person's journey of faith.

You should NOT try to prove the other person wrong, or convert them on the spot. Your arguments, no matter how good they are, will not change someone else's mind. Only they, with God's grace, can do that. Perhaps your openness about your faith will play a role in God's plan, but much of the time we do not see the immediate effects of the part we play.

Try to set up and maintain a dialog in which to argue points of faith - not a personal quarrel. Always refrain from making personal attacks or criticizing another's beliefs, even if they are overly critical of yours. Avoid hostile discussions, and walk away if the discussion is deteriorating into a quarrel.

Attitude is everything in Guerrilla Apologetics. If you fail to exercise tact and civility, your actions and tone will overshadow and taint your efforts. Ask questions with sincere curiosity, and respect the other person as an expert on their faith. After all, you would be offended if a non-Catholic accused you of not knowing your own faith, so do not make the same assumption about them. Your sensitivity and understanding to others beliefs will often lead them to exercise similar sensitivity and understanding. Remember, they believe what they do at least as strongly as you believe what you profess.

Most importantly, keep your friendship intact – if the discussion becomes too heated with a friend, take some time away from the subject.

The following conversation illustrates the Guerrilla Apologetics method:

Let's assume that in the usual course of business at school, at work, or around the neighborhood someone approaches you and asks, "You're Catholic, right? Why do you believe ..."

Answer their question to the best of your ability. While it is helpful when answering questions to have read up on your Hahn and Keating[*], not all of us can keep so much information mentally accessible, if we can memorize it at all. Take a deep breath, say a quick prayer, and think about your answer before you say it. Think your answer through; terminology is everything and a slip of the tongue can make your message more difficult to understand.

If you don't have the answer ready, or honestly don't know, go ahead and admit it. Let the other person know that you'll look into it and get back to them. When you get a chance use one or more of the resources found at the end of this book to find the answer. You can say something like, "That's a good question, but I don't have the answer now. I'll make sure I can get a proper explanation for you later."

---

[*] See the Recommended Resources at the end of the book

It is helpful to remember that the answer to a Biblical challenge can often be found near the challenge. More than once I have seen a challenger's argument refuted by the reading of their chosen quote in context.

If you do have an answer, keep it as brief as possible. Give them the reason you (as a Catholic) believe what you do. Most, if not all of the time, the question will be a misunderstanding that you will have to clear up. Do so courteously; while the other person may not have understood what they were asking about, no one likes to be told they are wrong, or for a big deal to be made out of their ignorance.

Once you have made a response, either a refutation, clarification, or a promise to find an answer for them, proceed to ask them a question. Lead in with something like:

"While we're discussing our beliefs, what do you believe about..."

How you ask this first question is important; especially since your challenger may not be prepared for a Catholic to inquire about *their* beliefs.

Do not interrupt them if they start to ask another question immediately after you respond to their first question, let them finish and then ask if you can ask a question before answering their second one.

Also, do not presume to know what you are talking about regarding what they believe – after all, most inquiries made of Catholics are based on misconceptions, it would be

7

unfortunate if Catholic questions were as misguided. In addition, with so many denominations of Christianity with so little emphasis on central teaching authority, it is very hard to predict what someone believes, even if they do affiliate themselves with a particular denomination. So do not accuse them in your question – ask, "What do you believe regarding confession?" instead of, "Why don't you believe in the institution of confession?" (especially since there are a good many non-Catholic Christians who do believe in the apostolic power to forgive sins!)

The questions given in each section of this book are worded to be open-ended, so feel free to use them as a guide in formulating questions to ask. Following each question is further background for reference – including the text or summary of any Biblical reference for convenience.

Once you have asked a question, give your challenger time to respond. Again, they may be surprised that you have challenged them, and they may not be familiar with the subject matter you have brought up. If the pause gets rather long and awkward, or they seem lost, give them a way out by saying, "If you're not sure, that's O.K., I was just curious. Did you have another question for me?" If they had asked a second question, remind them of it so they can resume the conversation easily. A question that stumps them may have the great impact, but if you relieve their awkwardness kindly, your attitude could be the greatest argument that Catholics are Christians after all.

While you will be challenging them to re-examine their beliefs, which they may find uncomfortable, do your best to make them feel comfortable in discussing their beliefs, and asking you about yours. Do your best to alternate asking questions and responding to questions, and always maintain a sense of calm, even if your challenger gets emotional.

If you happen to get into a debate with someone who you can not maintain a conversation with, such as someone who incessantly preaches to you, criticizes your beliefs repeatedly, or simply will not give you a chance to get a word in edgewise, excuse yourself and try to get some distance from them, at least for the moment. Not everyone will be receptive to an open discussion, and there is no point to tying to speak with someone who will not listen. Perhaps at some other time they will be more open to a conversation about their religious beliefs.

Again, remember that a personal relationship, even with co-workers, acquaintances, and enemies, is far more important than winning a debate. The manner in which you conduct yourself and treat others is far more powerful than any argument, however witty and true it is.

Question 1: Where in the Bible does it say the Bible is the only source of God's Revelation?

My wife was recently in a local Christian bookstore and inquired about a book by G.K. Chesterton, whose writings have been credited as having influenced the conversion of C.S. Lewis, among others, to Christianity. The clerk responded that they did not carry his works, as his writings were not based on Scripture. (Oddly enough, when I visited the store months later they featured a selection of "Hello Kitty" videos, though I am at a loss as to their scriptural basis.)

The store's rejection of anything non-scriptural is a reflection of the Protestant idea of **Sola Scriptura**, or Scripture Alone. The principle that Scripture is the sole revelation of God is a paradox, as the principle is neither found nor supported in the Bible.

The questioning of **Sola Scriptura** was a turning point for Scott Hahn, a convert to Catholicism and now an outspoken apologist and theologian. Thus, this is the first Guerrilla Apologetics question for your Protestant friends – Where in the Bible does it say the Bible is the only source of divine revelation?

For follow-up material, there is quite a bit – much of it Scriptural, in fact. Did Peter really only write two letters, or were Matthew, Mark, Luke and John the only followers to write their accounts of the life and teachings of Jesus? You can even point out where these Gospel writers attested to the numerous accounts and details that are not bound up in what we now call the Bible.

Luke begins his Gospel account by explaining why he decided to write it:

"Since many have undertaken to compile a narrative of the events that have been fulfilled among us, just as those who were eyewitnesses from the beginning and ministers of the word have handed down to us, I too have decided after investigating everything accurately anew, to write it down in an orderly sequence for you, most excellent Theophilus, so that you may realize the certainty of the teachings you have received." (Luke 1:1-4)

If "many" had already "compiled narratives," or written Gospels by the time Luke did, why are only three others in the Bible? If the eyewitnesses and "ministers to the word" had been handing their accounts down, how were they doing so without the Bible?

John's Gospel also testifies to the lack of a complete account of Jesus' life, as he states in the closing of his Gospel:

"Now Jesus did many other signs in the presence of His disciples that are not written in this book. But these are written that you may come to believe that Jesus is the

Messiah, the Son of God, and that through this belief you may have life in His name." (John 20:30-31)

"There are also many other things that Jesus did, but if these were to be described individually, I do not think the whole world would contain the books that could be written." (John 21:25)

Certainly John would not then believe that only 4 accounts of Jesus' life would be sufficient to encompass all of the details of His works, ministry, and teachings.

What teachings did Paul refer to when he told the early followers of Christ, "Therefore, brothers, stand firm and hold fast to the **traditions** that you were taught, either by **oral statement** or by a letter of ours." (2 Thessalonians 2:15)

Or, "And what you **heard from me** through many witnesses entrust to faithful people who will have the ability to teach others as well."(2 Tim 2:2)

Or, "Thus faith comes from what is **heard**, and what is **heard** comes through the word of Christ."(Rom 10:17)

Or, "I praise you because you remember me in everything and hold fast to the **traditions**, just as I handed them on to you." (1 Corinthians 11:2)

Or, "The word of the Lord remains forever. This is the word that has been **proclaimed** to you." (1 Peter 1:25)

Certainly Peter and Paul could not be referring to Luke's Gospel, as Luke did not write until years after their ministry, or of John's Revelations, the last book of the New Testament to be written. And what of the "oral statements" to which Christians are told to "hold fast?" These are to be followed as well as written works – and the Bible itself contains this instruction to heed both oral instruction and written teachings!

The Bible is a collection of writings by authors who did not write with the intention of their works being used in a compilation. I have had several Protestant friends refer to Revelations 22:18-19, "I warn everyone who hears the prophetic words in this book: if anyone adds to them, God will add to him the plagues described in this book, and if anyone takes away from the words in the prophetic book, God will take away his share in the tree of life and in the holy city described in this book." They claim that John was referring to the Bible, but how is this possible if John wrote Revelations in approximately AD 81-96, and it was not until 393 AD that the Council of Hippo first compiled the New Testament from all of the first-century Christian writings?

Of course if one is to be charged with "taking away" from the Bible, what does the Protestant think of Luther, who removed several books from the Bible as part of his break from the Church? While Protestants accuse the Catholic Church of adding books to the Bible, one only needs to compare the Catholic and Protestant Bibles to a pre-Reformation text, such as John Gutenberg's first printed Bible, to realize who added or subtracted from the Scriptures.

Indeed, with so much emphasis on a *book* as the Word of God, when the Scriptures point out that the Word of God became flesh and dwelt among us, and that His works were too numerous to be contained in all the books in the world, the Protestant idea of **Sola Scriptura** is dangerously close to, if it is not already, idolatry of the Bible.

However, as the Scriptures are a sacred text to all Christians, and most Protestants stake their entire religious belief system on the Bible alone, much of the Guerrilla Apologetics arguments will be based on Biblical references. If a Protestant asserts the Bible is to be taken literally, or is the only source of God's word, remind him of his admission as you ask Guerrilla Apologetics questions on various topics.

Question 2: Where in the Bible does it say faith or personal acceptance of Jesus is enough for Salvation?

Another pillar of Protestant Christianity is salvation by faith alone, or **Sola Fide**. This principle, in a nutshell, is that if one simply accepts Jesus as their personal Lord and Savior, they are "saved" by faith alone. Some Protestants even go so far as to criticize those who claim that one must also do good on earth – for they say such ideas are not scriptural.

Again, this is not a Biblical idea. When Nicodemus asked Jesus what he meant by being "born from above," Jesus responded: "Amen, Amen, I say to you, no one can enter the Kingdom of God without being born of **water and spirit**." (John 3:5) Baptism is a requirement for salvation according to Jesus, not just faith in Him.

In Matthew 25:32-46 Jesus compares the judgment of the world to the separation of goats from sheep. The sheep are blessed, and invited into the heavenly kingdom, for as they performed good works for "the least of My brothers," they honored Christ. The goats, on the other hand, **although they address Jesus as Lord** (verse 44) are condemned to "eternal punishment" because they did not perform works of mercy while they were on earth.

The epistle of James is perhaps the most profound in challenging **Sola Fide** – in fact, Martin Luther referred to it as "an epistle of straw," and almost removed it along with the Old Testament texts now found only in our Catholic versions of the Bible. What was it that threatened this pillar of Protestantism?

"What good is it, my brothers, if someone says he has faith but does not have works? Can that faith save him? If a brother or sister has nothing to wear and has no food for the day, and one of you says to them, 'Go in peace, keep warm, and eat well,' but you do not give them the necessities of the body, what good is it? So faith of itself, if it does not have works, is dead." (James 2:14-17)

The chapter continues to expound on the idea, which James considers so important that he is quite stern with the reader:

"You believe that God is one. You do well. Even the demons believe that and tremble. Do you want proof, you ignoramus, that faith without works is useless? Was not Abraham our father justified by works when he offered his son Isaac upon the altar? You see that faith was active along with his works, and faith was completed by the works. See how **a person is justified by works and not faith alone**. For just as a body without a spirit is dead, so also faith without works is dead." (James 2:19-22,24,26)

Salvation is also not something once attained and never lost. Rather, it is in need of constant upkeep, according to Paul:

"Therefore, my dear friends, as you have always obeyed–not only in my presence, but now much more in my absence–continue to work out your salvation with fear and trembling." (Philippians 2:12)

Jesus also gave the example of the "faithful and prudent" steward, who is punished severely and given a place among the unfaithful after he sins in the absence of his master. (Luke 12:42-46)

Consider also Jesus' discourse on the vine and the branches in John 15:1-6. He likens Himself to the vine, and His followers to branches. However, "Anyone who does not remain in Me will be thrown out like a branch and wither; people will gather them and throw them into a fire and they will be burned." (John 15:6)

Of course, to see that salvation can be had and lost, and regained again, consider our first parents, Adam and Eve, and the Biblical account of how they were created sinless and in fellowship with God, but through doubt and disobedience they lost their grace.

Does the fall of Adam and Eve (Genesis 3) support the "Once saved, always saved" teaching?

Question 3: Who founded your church?

I remember seeing a Peanuts cartoon in which Charlie Brown was watching his sister Sally write a report on Church history. "To write about Church history," she begins, "one must go back to the very beginning." She begins the second sentence, "Our pastor was born in 1930…"

The comic is funny because we realize that the founding of a single church by a man is not "the very beginning." Yet for Protestants, this is the case of those who follow Luther (the Lutherans), Henry VIII (Anglicans and Episcopalians), John Smyth (Baptists), John Knox (Presbyterians), and John and Charles Wesley (Methodists), to name only a few.

But the Catholic Church does not refer back to just any man as its founder, but Jesus Christ – indeed, if you follow a Protestant church's history back, beyond the pastor, beyond the founder, you find its separation from the Catholic Church (or from another church that had separated from the Catholic Church).

Here are some of the major denominations and the year of their founding (sometimes approximated). Note the irony that the dates are measured, more or less, from the founding of the Catholic Church by Christ.

1517 – Lutherans (Martin Luther)

1534 – Anglican (England) / Episcopalian (US) (Henry VIII)

1560 – Presbyterian (John Knox)

1600 – Baptist (John Smyth)

1652 – Friends/Quaker (George Fox)

1739 – Methodist (John and Charles Wesley)

1830 – Mormon (Joseph Smith)

1865 – Salvation Army (William Booth)

1870 – Jehovah's Witnesses (Charles Taze Russell)

1879 – Christian Science (Mary Baker Eddy)

1900 – Pentecostal (No clear date of founding or evidence of a particular founder, but several movements appeared in the early 1900s, generally with backgrounds in other denominations)

Question 4: (a)Do you Interpret the Bible for yourself? (b)Does your church teach with the Authority of Christ?

No Christian seems to doubt the validity of the Bible, but what of its interpretation? Peter plainly states, "There is no prophecy in scripture that is a matter of personal interpretation." (2 Peter 3:16)

As to the letters of Paul, Peter cautions, "In them there are some things hard to understand that the ignorant and unstable distort to their own destruction, just as they do the other scriptures." (2 Peter 3:16)

The most famous "distortion" of Scripture, or its meaning, is the temptation of Jesus by the devil, who cites Psalm 91 in an effort to lure Jesus into testing God:

"Then the devil took Him to the holy city, and made Him stand on the parapet of the temple, and said to Him, 'If you are the Son of God, throw yourself down. For it is written, "He will command his angels concerning you," and "with their hands they will support you, lest you dash your foot against a stone."'" (Matthew 4:5-6).

If even Satan twists scripture to his own ends, how is a human to interpret the Bible without error? Even Peter (in the Bible) says that the texts themselves can be easily misunderstood.

Jesus did establish an authoritative church on earth to teach, and as He did not remain physically on earth to lead it, He appointed a human leader and foundation for this church:

"Blessed are you, Simon son of Jonah. For flesh and blood has not revealed this to you, but My heavenly Father. And so I say to you, you are Peter, and upon this rock I will build My church, and the gates of the netherworld shall not prevail against it. I will give you the keys to the kingdom of heaven. Whatever you bind on earth shall be bound in heaven, whatever you loose on earth shall be loosed in heaven." (Matthew 16:17-19)

Significance is added when one realizes that Jesus speaks of a church only twice in the Gospels – here in His declaration that Peter is the foundation of an earthly church, and later in Matthew 18:17 when it is said that the church acts as a judge of a sinner – the power of binding and loosing is again mentioned, after stating that one who refuses to listen to the church is to be cut off – "treated as you would a Gentile or tax collector."

It should be noted that many Protestants will point out that the Greek words for "rock" were used in two different genders, "petros" and "petra," and Greek texts quote Jesus as saying, "You are Petros (sometimes meaning 'piece of rock,' or 'small rock'), and upon this petra (rock) I will build my church." This appears to portray Jesus as distinguishing Peter from the foundation of the church (although in Greek, using a feminine noun "petra" as a man's name would be improper). However, Jesus did not speak Greek, He spoke Aramaic, the local language, and much of the early Christian writings were likewise first written in Aramaic, then translated into Greek. In Aramaic, there is only one word for rock - "kephas."

While the argument that Jesus spoke Aramaic, and thus used the Aramaic word "kephas" is a common defensive apologetical argument, let me point out the guerrilla way to address the topic – ask your friend, "What did the followers of Christ call Simon, Kephas or Petros?"

Paul, who wrote often in Greek, refers to "Peter" only once, in 2 Gal 2, 7-8. He refers to "Kephas" much more often – four times in 1 Corinthians (1,12; 3,22; 9,5;15,4) and twice in 1 Galatians (1,18; 2, 9-14).

1 John does refer to "Petros" once (1,42), but the overwhelming use of the Aramaic "Kephas" begs the question – why do Protestants persist in believing Christ used the two Greek words to distinguish Peter from the foundation of His church? In the Bible, even Paul refers to Peter's Aramaic name "Kephas" – of which there is only one form, and one definition. It certainly appears that Paul acknowledged Peter was Kephas, *the* kephas upon which Christ established his church on earth.

We are all familiar with the parable of the Good Shepherd (John 10:1-16), in which Jesus calls Himself the shepherd. "They will hear my voice, and there will be one flock, one shepherd," He says. Later in the same Gospel account, after the resurrection, Jesus asks Peter three times, "Do you love Me?" After Peter answers "Yes" three times, Jesus replies, "Feed my lambs," and then "Feed my sheep." The one shepherd directed Peter, the foundation of His church, to also care for the "one flock"- in addition to making him the "rock" upon which He built His church, a church with the power to bind and loose, declaring persistent sinners to be outside the church community (or, ex-communicated).

By the way, the idea of the Church leadership caring for the "one flock" of Jesus was believed in the early Church, even after Jesus' ascension. In his first letter, Peter revisits the metaphor of the shepherding of the Church, when he admonishes leaders to, "Tend the flock of God in your midst ... And when the Chief Shepherd is revealed, you will receive the unfading crown of glory." (1 Peter 5:2,4)

Do Protestants exhibit the authority of which Jesus spoke? Hardly. By emphasizing private interpretation and belittling the idea of one disciple being named the foundation of Christ's church, Protestant denominations have denied their own church leaders the authority to teach with authority – and when an issue divides a church, such as the ordination of homosexuals, the churches built on sand cannot hold the flock together. Leaders of these churches do not exhibit, or even claim, to have the authority of Jesus, who told his disciples, "Whoever listens to you, listens to Me. Whoever rejects you rejects Me. And whoever rejects Me rejects the One who sent Me." (Luke 10:16)

Returning to the original question, how can one interpret correctly? One can look to the authority on earth that Christ established! Jesus promised that the "gates of the netherworld would not prevail" against His church when He first called Simon, "Kephas," the rock. If an error were to occur in the teaching of that church, Jesus' promise would be broken. The disciples, and their successors, are guided by the Spirit of truth (John 14:17) promised by Jesus: "the holy Spirit that the Father will send in My name – He will teach you everything and remind you of all that I told you." (John 14:26)

Question 5: Does your church trace its leadership directly back to Christ?

This question is a good follow-up to the ones listed earlier regarding the founding and authority of non-Catholic Christian churches.

Can your challenger trace the leadership of their church all the way back to the promise made to Peter that death (or hell, depending on the translation of the Bible used) would not prevail against the Church? Do they believe Christ left His Church on earth without a visible leader or physical, present authority to correct errors for so many generations? If so, what became of the promise for a Church founded on a rock that death (or hell) could not overcome?

The following is a list of every pope from Peter to Benedict XVI, who reigned at the time this book was written. Its length is a testimony to the unbroken lineage and promise of the papacy.

1. St. Peter (32-67)
2. St. Linus (67-76)
3. St. Anacletus (Cletus) (76-88)
4. St. Clement I (88-97)
5. St. Evaristus (97-105)
6. St. Alexander I (105-115)
7. St. Sixtus I (Xystus I) (115-125)
8. St. Telesphorus (125-136)
9. St. Hyginus (136-140)
10. St. Pius I (140-155)
11. St. Anicetus (155-166)
12. St. Soter (166-175)

13. St. Eleutherius (175-189)
14. St. Victor I (189-199)
15. St. Zephyrinus (199-217)
16. St. Callistus I (217-22)
17. St. Urban I (222-30)
18. St. Pontain (230-35)
19. St. Anterus (235-36)
20. St. Fabian (236-50)
21. St. Cornelius (251-53)
22. St. Lucius I (253-54)
23. St. Stephen I (254-257)
24. St. Sixtus II (257-258)
25. St. Dionysius (260-268)
26. St. Felix I (269-274)
27. St. Eutychian (275-283)
28. St. Caius (Gaius)(283-296)
29. St. Marcellinus (296-304)
30. St. Marcellus I (308-309)
31. St. Eusebius (309 or 310)
32. St. Miltiades (311-14)
33. St. Sylvester I (314-35)
34. St. Marcus (336)
35. St. Julius I (337-52)
36. Liberius (352-66)
37. St. Damasus I (366-83)
38. St. Siricius (384-99)
39. St. Anastasius I (399-401)
40. St. Innocent I (401-17)
41. St. Zosimus (417-18)
42. St. Boniface I (418-22)
43. St. Celestine I (422-32)
44. St. Sixtus III (432-40)
45. St. Leo I (the Great) (440-61)
46. St. Hilarius (461-68)

47.St. Simplicius (468-83)
48.St. Felix III (II) (483-92)
49.St. Gelasius I (492-96)
50.Anastasius II (496-98)
51.St. Symmachus (498-514)
52.St. Hormisdas (514-23)
53.St. John I (523-26)
54.St. Felix IV (III) (526-30)
55.Boniface II (530-32)
56.John II (533-35)
57.St. Agapetus I (Agapitus I) (535-36)
58.St. Silverius (536-37)
59.Vigilius (537-55)
60.Pelagius I (556-61)
61.John III (561-74)
62.Benedict I (575-79)
63.Pelagius II (579-90)
64.St. Gregory I (the Great) (590-604)
65.Sabinian (604-606)
66.Boniface III (607)
67.St. Boniface IV (608-15)
68.St. Deusdedit (Adeodatus I) (615-18)
69.Boniface V (619-25)
70.Honorius I (625-38)
71.Severinus (640)
72.John IV (640-42)
73.Theodore I (642-49)
74.St. Martin I (649-55)
75.St. Eugene I (655-57)
76.St. Vitalian (657-72)
77.Adeodatus (II) (672-76)
78.Donus (676-78)
79.St. Agatho (678-81)
80.St. Leo II (682-83)

81.St. Benedict II (684-85)
82.John V (685-86)
83.Conon (686-87)
84.St. Sergius I (687-701)
85.John VI (701-05)
86.John VII (705-07)
87.Sisinnius (708)
88.Constantine (708-15)
89.St. Gregory II (715-31)
90.St. Gregory III (731-41)
91.St. Zachary (741-52)
   Stephen II (752) (Died before he was consecrated as Pope)
92.Stephen III (752-57)
93.St. Paul I (757-67)
94.Stephen IV (767-72)
95.Adrian I (772-95)
96.St. Leo III (795-816)
97.Stephen V (816-17)
98.St. Paschal I (817-24)
99.Eugene II (824-27)
100.Valentine (827)
101.Gregory IV (827-44)
102.Sergius II (844-47)
103.St. Leo IV (847-55)
104.Benedict III (855-58)
105.St. Nicholas I (the Great) (858-67)
106.Adrian II (867-72)
107.John VIII (872-82)
108.Marinus I (882-84)
109.St. Adrian III (884-85)
110.Stephen VI (885-91)
111.Formosus (891-96)
112.Boniface VI (896)
113.Stephen VII (896-97)

114.Romanus (897)
115.Theodore II (897)
116.John IX (898-900)
117.Benedict IV (900-03)
118.Leo V (903)
119.Sergius III (904-11)
120.Anastasius III (911-13)
121.Lando (913-14)
122.John X (914-28)
123.Leo VI (928)
124.Stephen VIII (929-31)
125.John XI (931-35)
126.Leo VII (936-39)
127.Stephen IX (939-42)
128.Marinus II (942-46)
129.Agapetus II (946-55)
130.John XII (955-63)
131.Leo VIII (963-64)
132.Benedict V (964)
133.John XIII (965-72)
134.Benedict VI (973-74)
135.Benedict VII (974-83)
136.John XIV (983-84)
137.John XV (985-96)
138.Gregory V (996-99)
139.Sylvester II (999-1003)
140.John XVII (1003)
141.John XVIII (1003-09)
142.Sergius IV (1009-12)
143.Benedict VIII (1012-24)
144.John XIX (1024-32)
145.Benedict IX (1032-45)
146.Sylvester III (1045)
147.Benedict IX (1045)

148.Gregory VI (1045-46)
149.Clement II (1046-47)
150.Benedict IX (1047-48)
151.Damasus II (1048)
152.St. Leo IX (1049-54)
153.Victor II (1055-57)
154.Stephen X (1057-58)
155.Nicholas II (1058-61)
156.Alexander II (1061-73)
157.St. Gregory VII (1073-85)
158.Blessed Victor III (1086-87)
159.Blessed Urban II (1088-99)
160.Paschal II (1099-1118)
161.Gelasius II (1118-19)
162.Callistus II (1119-24)
163.Honorius II (1124-30)
164.Innocent II (1130-43)
165.Celestine II (1143-44)
166.Lucius II (1144-45)
167.Blessed Eugene III (1145-53)
168.Anastasius IV (1153-54)
169.Adrian IV (1154-59)
170.Alexander III (1159-81)
171.Lucius III (1181-85)
172.Urban III (1185-87)
173.Gregory VIII (1187)
174.Clement III (1187-91)
175.Celestine III (1191-98)
176.Innocent III (1198-1216)
177.Honorius III (1216-27)
178.Gregory IX (1227-41)
179.Celestine IV (1241)
180.Innocent IV (1243-54)
181.Alexander IV (1254-61)

182.Urban IV (1261-64)
183.Clement IV (1265-68)
184.Blessed Gregory X (1271-76)
185.Blessed Innocent V (1276)
186.Adrian V (1276)
187.John XXI (1276-77)
188.Nicholas III (1277-80)
189.Martin IV (1281-85)
190.Honorius IV (1285-87)
191.Nicholas IV (1288-92)
192.St. Celestine V (1294)
193.Boniface VIII (1294-1303)
194.Blessed Benedict XI (1303-04)
195.Clement V (1305-14)
196.John XXII (1316-34)
197.Benedict XII (1334-42)
198.Clement VI (1342-52)
199.Innocent VI (1352-62)
200.Blessed Urban V (1362-70)
201.Gregory XI (1370-78)
202.Urban VI (1378-89)
203.Boniface IX (1389-1404)
204.Innocent VII (1404-06)
205.Gregory XII (1406-15)
206.Martin V (1417-31)
207.Eugene IV (1431-47)
208.Nicholas V (1447-55)
209.Callistus III (1455-58)
210.Pius II (1458-64)
211.Paul II (1464-71)
212.Sixtus IV (1471-84)
213.Innocent VIII (1484-92)
214.Alexander VI (1492-1503)
215.Pius III (1503)

216.Julius II (1503-13)
217.Leo X (1513-21)
218.Adrian VI (1522-23)
219.Clement VII (1523-34)
220.Paul III (1534-49)
221.Julius III (1550-55)
222.Marcellus II (1555)
223.Paul IV (1555-59)
224.Pius IV (1559-65)
225.St. Pius V (1566-72)
226.Gregory XIII (1572-85)
227.Sixtus V (1585-90)
228.Urban VII (1590)
229.Gregory XIV (1590-91)
230.Innocent IX (1591)
231.Clement VIII (1592-1605)
232.Leo XI (1605)
233.Paul V (1605-21)
234.Gregory XV (1621-23)
235.Urban VIII (1623-44)
236.Innocent X (1644-55)
237.Alexander VII (1655-67)
238.Clement IX (1667-69)
239.Clement X (1670-76)
240.Blessed Innocent XI (1676-89)
241.Alexander VIII (1689-91)
242.Innocent XII (1691-1700)
243.Clement XI (1700-21)
244.Innocent XIII (1721-24)
245.Benedict XIII (1724-30)
246.Clement XII (1730-40)
247.Benedict XIV (1740-58)
248.Clement XIII (1758-69)
249.Clement XIV (1769-74)

250.Pius VI (1775-99)
251.Pius VII (1800-23)
252.Leo XII (1823-29)
253.Pius VIII (1829-30)
254.Gregory XVI (1831-46)
255.Blessed Pius IX (1846-78)
256.Leo XIII (1878-1903)
257.St. Pius X (1903-14)
258.Benedict XV (1914-22)
259.Pius XI (1922-39)
260.Pius XII (1939-58)
261.Blessed John XXIII (1958-63)
262.Paul VI (1963-78)
263.John Paul I (1978)
264.John Paul II (1978-2005)
265.Benedict XVI (2005—)

It may be noted that among the saints there are also less savory characters among the popes. Keep in mind that the first Pope, hand-picked by Jesus, denied Him three times. Jesus, knowing Peter's weakness, still found him worthy of serving as the head of the Church – how can we consider Peter's successors unworthy of the office for doing less treacherous wrongs?

Of all the papal scandals in the Catholic Church, none have been as terrible as the first Pope flatly denying even knowing Jesus. Since this was done by Jesus' hand-picked representative, how can we criticize the papacy based on the failings of the men who have served in the office?

Question 6: **Does your church recognize specific individuals to be held up as examples?**

Leaders of the early Church sought to have members follow examples not only of Christ, but of others who lived their lives in accordance with His teachings.

"**Join with others in being imitators of me**, brothers, and observe those who thus conduct themselves **according to the model** you have in us." (Phillipians 3:17)

"**Be imitators of me, as I am of Christ.**" (1 Corinthians 11:1-3)

"**Take as an example** of hardship and patience, brothers, the prophets who spoke in the name of the Lord. **Indeed, we call blessed those who have persevered**. " (James 5:10-11)

Members of the early Church were likewise called to be examples to each other, as well as those to whom they preached the Gospel.

"Let no one have contempt for your youth, but **set an example for those who believe**, in speech, conduct, love, faith, and purity." (1 Timothy 4:12)

"Tend the flock of God in your midst, not by constraint but willingly, as God would have it, not for shameful profit but eagerly. Do not lord it over those assigned to you, but **be examples to the flock**." (1 Peter 5:2-3)

Other Christian churches will laud the idea of using individuals as examples, but at the same time condemn Catholics for doing the same with saints. This makes no sense, as the Catholic Church goes to great lengths to validate the character and standing of an individual to the status of saint in order to ensure that the person is indeed someone to be emulated.

In a nutshell, the process includes a five-year waiting period, an investigation commissioned by the local bishop, review of the case by theologians, cardinals, and bishops. A miracle connected to the individual must be observed and verified after their death, a key requirement for Beatification. Once beatified, an individual may be used as an example for the Church within a limited scope. A second miracle, which must have occurred following the Beatification at the request of someone who sought the Beatified individual's intercession, is a necessary part of the process to canonize the person, or declare them officially a saint, worthy of following as an example.

Ask your challenger if they have ever asked a friend, pastor, or anyone to pray for them. Explain that in doing so, they were asking the person to intercede on their behalf to God. Ask why they did, and one answer may be because they "knew God listened to that person." How did they know? Did they take five years reviewing the person's life, and thoroughly investigate at least two miracles attributed to the person before considering them helpful in petitioning God? Probably not.

Another practice to ask your challenger is whether they keep photos of loved ones in their home or in their purse or wallet. If they do, point out that we Catholics keep images of our heroes, the exemplary saints, around us to remind us of what they have done, and the things that we must do to serve God. Certainly they do not believe a picture of their children to actually *BE* their children, and neither do we Catholics believe a statue or relic to *BE* the actual saint, but rather a sacred and treasured reminder of someone the Church knows to be loved by God.

Notice that the last two paragraphs are actually defensive arguments. However, when phrased as a question about what the person practices and believes, followed by a similar Catholic practice, they become arguments for being Catholic.

This section cannot be complete without discussing the greatest among the saints honored by Catholics, Mary. It is difficult to build a case for being Catholic on her, as the honor given to Mary as "Mother of God" and the "Mediatrix" is not easily understood by other Christians. Even Kimberly Hahn, in her testimony about her road to Catholicism, admitted that understanding the high honor attributed to Mary was one of the last hurdles she had to reconcile before coming to the Catholic Church.

Yet while Mary may be a difficult subject to use in evangelization, to some outside the Church her importance to Catholics can be strikingly understood.

David Neff, editor of Christianity Today observed that the movie The Passion of the Christ had a profound impact on on non-Catholic Christian women, particularly for the role May played.

"Hail, thou that art highly favored, the Lord is with thee: blessed art thou among women." (Luke 1:28, KJV)
"Blessed art thou among women, and blessed is the fruit of thy womb!" (Luke 1:42, KJV)

Do these verses sound anything like a certain Marian prayer?

"After both of *The Passion* screenings I attended, the Protestant women talked about identifying with Mary as a mother who was watching her child suffer," said Neff in an article titled *Mel, Mary, and Mothers* in the March 2004 issue of *Christianity Today*. "From whatever point in his spirituality [Mel] Gibson's treatment of Mary is springing, it is touching deeply the maternal impulse in his viewers."

As an example, the Bible gives many reasons for Jesus' earthly mother to be praised.

When the angel appears to Mary to announce her role as earthly mother to God's Son, he greets her with praise:

"And coming to her, he [the angel] said, '**Hail, favored one, the Lord is with you**.' But she was greatly troubled at what was said and pondered what kind of greeting this might be. Then the angel said to her, 'Do not be afraid, Mary, for **you have found favor with God**.'" (Luke 1:28-30)

When Mary visits her cousin Elizabeth, she is greeted with praise there as well:

"[Elizabeth] cried out in a loud voice, '**Most blessed are you among women**, and blessed is the fruit of your womb. And how does this happen to me, that **the mother of my Lord** should come to me? For at the moment the sound of your greeting reached my ears, the infant in my womb lept for joy. **Blessed are you who believed** that what was spoken to you by the Lord would be fulfilled.'" (Luke 1:42-45)

Mary responds, recognizing the honor that has been bestowed on her, and that she will be referred to as blessed for what God has done:

"And Mary said: 'My soul proclaims the greatness of the Lord; my spirit rejoices in God my savior. For he has looked upon his handmaid's lowliness; **behold, from now on will all ages call me blessed**. The Mighty One has done great things for me, and holy is His name'" (Luke 1:46-49)

Mary recognized that without God, she was nothing, but because of God having chosen her, she had received honor, and would be called blessed. Note also that much of the "Hail Mary" is taken from these passages in the first chapter of Luke's Gospel (though the wording varies based on the translation). As she accepted and assented to the angel's tidings, she is an exemplary model for Christians.

So the Bible tells us Mary is blessed, and will be called blessed, and by her obedience she is a good example. But what of her ability to intercede on our behalf?

In John 2 the story of the wedding feast at Cana is told. When the wine runs out, it is Mary that speaks to her son. Though at first it seems Jesus will not get involved, in the end He follows His mother's prompting:

"When the wine ran short, the mother of Jesus said to Him, 'They have no wine.'
    'Jesus said to her, 'Woman, how does your concern affect me? My hour has not yet come.'
    His mother said to the servers, 'Do whatever He tells you.'" (John 2:3-5)

So if Jesus performed His first miracle after his mother intercedes for the bride and groom, we Catholics find a Biblical root for asking Mary to intercede for us.

On a final note, Mary's command to the servants is the last quote of hers found in the Bible – a motherly command to all of us that no Christian can deny is valid: "Do whatever He tells you."

Jesus performed his first miracle after His mother interceded for the bride and groom in Cana. Is there any reason to think she has ceased to intercede for others?

Question 7: Do ministers of your church forgive sins in Jesus' name?

Question 4 dealt with authority in Christ's Church. Another passage that speaks of the granting of authority to the disciples is John 20:21:

"Jesus said to them again, 'Peace be with you. As the Father has sent me, so I send you,'" identifying His mission on earth with their new mission – one of authoritative teaching and forgiveness.

The next verses, 22 and 23, go as follows:

"And then when He had said this, He breathed on them and said to them, 'Receive the holy Spirit. Whose sins you forgive are forgiven them, and whose sins you retain are retained.'"

Now consider that he granted the disciples the power to heal the sick and drive out demons (Luke 10:9,17-19), and they were able to do so in His name.

Finally, recall that the scribes challenged Jesus when he forgave the sins of the paralytic in Mark 2:1-12. "Why does this man speak this way? He is blaspheming," they said of Jesus.

Jesus asked in reply, "Which is easier, to say to the paralytic 'Your sins are forgiven,' or 'Rise, pick up your mat and go home?'" He then said the latter to the paralytic, who was immediately cured.

If, as Jesus says, it is easier to forgive sins than to heal the lame ...

Therefore:

1) The Bible tells us Jesus gave His disciples the power to heal, and tells us that they were able to do so in His name.
2) The Bible states that Jesus also granted the disciples the power to forgive men's sins.
3) Finally, in the Bible Jesus demonstrated to the Pharisees that the power to forgive sins was "easier" than the power to heal.

How can we doubt the Bible's statement that Jesus granted the disciples the ability to forgive sins in His name?

... Can we deny either power to His apostles, since He explicitly gave them both abilities, and there is Biblically documented proof that the Apostles exercised the more difficult power? (as they did in Acts 3:1-8)

Question 8: What is your church's teaching about Purgatory?

We Catholics have been attacked for our beliefs on Purgatory, but it is possible to use it as an argument for Catholicism, instead of trying to explain our belief.

Much of the criticism of teachings on Purgatory are based on misconceptions; it is not a "second chance" for salvation, but a passage of purification.

There are many Biblical statements that support a period of forgiveness or purification after death, or at least a chance of forgiveness:

"Therefore, I say to you, every sin and blasphemy will be forgiven people, blasphemy against the Spirit will not be forgiven. And whoever speaks a word against the Son of Man will be forgiven; but whoever speaks against the holy Spirit will not be forgiven, **either in this age or in the age to come**. " (Matthew 12:31-33)

Depending on the translation, some Bibles phrase the last statement as "in this life or the next." If Heaven and Hell are the only places souls go, is it in Hell that they find forgiveness, or are they admitted, sinful, into Heaven and later forgiven?

Praying for those who have died is also found in the Scriptures:

"May the Lord grant mercy to the family of Onesiphorus because he often gave me new heart and was not ashamed of my chains ... **May the Lord grant him to find mercy** from the Lord on that day, and you know very well the services he rendered in Ephesus." (2 Timothy 1:16,18)

Paul speaks of Onesiphorus as if he were dead – if so, what good would it be to pray for mercy for his deceased friend?

In the Old Testament, the story of Judas Maccabeus treating deceased Jews, later discovered to have lived in violation of God's law, shows that even before Christ's time there was a strong belief that the prayers of the living could help the dead.

"They [Judas and his soldiers] prayed that the sinful deed might be fully blotted out. ... He then took up a collection among all his soldiers, amounting to two thousand drachmas, which he sent to Jerusalem to provide for an expiatory sacrifice. **In doing this he acted in a very excellent and noble way**, inasmuch as he had the resurrection of the dead in view; for **if he were not expecting the fallen to rise again, it would have been useless and foolish to pray for them in death**. But if he did this with a view to the splendid reward that awaits those who had gone to rest in godliness, **it was a holy and pious thought. Thus he made atonement for the dead that they might be freed from this sin**. (2 Maccabees 12:40-46)

If we Christians claim to believe in the resurrection, ought we to perform such "holy and pious" acts such as praying for the dead? While Maccabees 1 and 2 are not found in non-Catholic Bibles, they are part of the pre-Reformation Bible. The fact that Paul sought mercy for his deceased friend is a sign that this belief was a part of the early

Church. This passage is very clear that one who believed in the resurrection would be wise to pray for the dead.

Peter, in his first letter, speaks of Jesus witnessing to those "in prison" specifically those who lived at the time of Noah. What was the purpose, or even the possibility, of the Gospel being preached to those in Hell? What would the point be of preaching to those in Heaven?

"For Christ also suffered for sins once, the righteous for the sake of the unrighteous, that He might lead you to God. Put to death in the flesh, he was brought to life in the spirit. In it **He also went to preach to the spirits in prison, who had once been disobedient** while God patiently waited in the days of Noah during the building of the ark..."(1 Peter 3:18-20)

"For this is why the gospel was preached even to the dead that, though condemned in the flesh in human estimation, they might live in the spirit in the estimation of God." (1 Peter 4:6)

Question 9: What does your church teach about divorce, and what did Jesus teach?

This is a sensitive subject, but a very clear commandment from Jesus that is ignored or explained away by Protestants who otherwise proclaim the Bible is to be taken literally.

Consider these words of Jesus:

"Have you not read that from the beginning the Creator 'made them male and female' and said, 'For this reason a man shall leave his father and mother and be joined to his wife, and the two shall become one flesh?' So they are no longer two, but one flesh. Therefore, what God has joined together, no human being must separate." (Mt 19:4-6)

When questioned about Moses' allowance of divorce, Jesus makes his point even clearer:

"Because of the hardness of your hearts Moses allowed you to divorce your wives, but from the beginning it was not so. I say to you, whoever divorces his wife (unless the marriage is unlawful) and marries another commits adultery." (Mt 19:8-9)

Jesus' declaration of divorce and remarriage as adultery is recorded in Mark's Gospel as well:

"Whoever divorces his wife and marries another commits adultery against her; and if she divorces her husband and marries another, she commits adultery." (Mark 10:11-12)

While many Protestant churches allow divorce and remarriage (with or without restrictions), it is clear that Jesus did not allow it, unless the marriage was deemed unlawful.

However, be tactful in making this argument, for there are many Christians who have been hurt in bad marriages and, without the Catholic Church to authoritatively declare the marriage unlawful (to declare it null as it already was in God's view), they have only had recourse to divorce.

Question 10: **What does your church teach about John 6:32-68 (the bread of life discourse) and/or the Gospel accounts of the last supper?**

This is, without a doubt, the single greatest issue to raise while discussing religion with Protestants. It is the ultimate Guerrilla Apologetics topic, and is especially convincing if the non-Catholic you are talking with has asserted that the Bible is to be taken literally.

John 3:16 is a popular one-verse summation of God's plan of salvation, according to Protestants:

"For God so loved the world that He gave His only Son, so that everyone who believes in Him might not perish but might have eternal life."

If Catholics were to hold up signs at sporting events and other public displays, the passage should be John 6:53-55:

"Jesus said to them, 'Amen, amen, I say to you, unless you eat of the flesh of the Son of Man and drink His blood, you do not have life within you. Whoever eats of My flesh and drinks My blood has eternal life, and I will raise Him on the last day. For My flesh is true food, and My blood is true drink."

So while Jesus came to earth so that those who believe "might have eternal life," they "do not have life within" "unless you eat of the flesh of the Son of Man and drink His blood."

Let us step back though, and look at the whole section – John 6:32-68 (I suggest you read the passages directly from your Bible, but have summarized the story here). Jesus had just fed the multitude on the previous day, and they had come looking for Him. Jesus assessed their motivation, seeking Him "not because you saw signs but because you ate the loaves and were filled." (John 6:26) They ask for a sign, and refer to the manna in the desert. Jesus responds:

"Amen, amen, I say to you, it was not Moses who gave you bread from heaven; My Father gives you the true bread from heaven. For the bread of God is that which comes down from heaven and gives life to the world."

When the crowd asks for this bread, Jesus responds:

"I am the bread of life; whoever comes to Me will never hunger, and whoever believes in Me shall never thirst."

The Jews, the Gospel says, murmured about this claim. Jesus then explains further:

"I am the living bread come down from heaven; whoever eats this bread will live forever; and the bread that I will give is My flesh for the life of the world."

When the Jews wonder how he can give his flesh to eat, Jesus responds in John 6:53-55 (as quoted before) that His flesh is true food, His blood real drink, and consummation is necessary for salvation.

Again, the Jews murmur, and some of his disciples leave. Bread was used symbolically in Passover meals, so bread as symbolism was not the concern. Jesus had repeatedly said that He would give his flesh to eat, flesh that was real food. He did not phrase it as a parable, He did not say, "I am like the bread of life," or "My flesh is like true food" – He used the word "is." Nor did he attempt to soften His teaching or change His wording – when disciples departed from Him, He turned to the twelve and asked them if they wanted to leave too. This was not optional teaching – this was to be accepted or rejected as the means to salvation. Five times in John 6:48-58 Jesus refers to eating the bread of life, His flesh. He repeats it without explaining away the idea as symbolism.

Now, let's jump forward to the Last Supper. Matthew, Mark, and Luke all give accounts of the breaking of the bread:

"While they were eating, Jesus took bread, said the blessing, broke it, and giving it to His disciples said, 'Take and eat; this is My Body.' Then He took a cup, gave thanks, and gave it to them saying, 'Drink from it, all of you, for this is My blood of the covenant, which will be shed on behalf of many for the forgiveness of sins.'" (Mt 26:26-28)

"While they were eating, He took bread, said the blessing, broke it, and gave it to them, and said, 'Take it; this is My body.' Then He took a cup, gave thanks, and gave it to them, and they all drank from it. 'This is My blood of the covenant, which will be shed for many.'" (Mark 14:22-24)

56

Christians cannot simply ignore the strong language in the Bread of Life Discourse (John 6) and its relation to the breaking of the bread at the Last Supper - accounts of which are present in three gospel accounts and St. Paul's first letter to the Corinthians.

"Then He took the bread, said the blessing, broke it, and gave it to them, saying, 'This is My body, which will be given for you; do this in memory of Me.' And likewise the cup after they had eaten, saying, 'This cup is the new covenant in My blood, which will be shed for you.'" (Luke 22:19-20)

St. Paul even addresses the Last Supper, and how it should be received in the Christian community:

"For I received from the Lord what I also handed on to you, that the Lord Jesus, on the night He was handed over, took bread, and, after he had given thanks, broke it and said, 'This is My body that is for you. Do this in remembrance of Me.' In the same way also the cup, after supper, saying, 'This cup is the new covenant in My blood. Do this, as often as you drink it, in remembrance of Me.' For as often as you eat this bread and drink the cup, you proclaim the death of the Lord until He comes.

Therefore whoever eats the bread or drinks the cup of the Lord unworthily will have to answer for the body and blood of the Lord. A person should examine himself, and so eat the bread and drink the cup. For anyone who eats and drinks without discerning the body eats and drinks judgment on himself." (1 Corinthians 11:23-29)

Note, once again, that in all four accounts Jesus does not speak as though it was a parable – He does not say, "This is like My body," or "This is a symbol of My blood." He says it *is* – and who are we to doubt His word?

All things were created through the Word, which became flesh. (John 1:3,14) Do we doubt that? Do we doubt that He could have made stones children of Abraham, or stones into bread? (Luke 3:8 ; Mt 4:3). If we believe the Bible, don't we also believe He changed water into wine? (John 2:1-12) How is it then, that a true "Christian," or believer in Christ, can doubt Jesus' ability to change the substance of bread and wine into His body and blood – especially after He said that His flesh was true food and His blood true drink – and eating and drinking His body and blood were requirements for eternal life?

When He who is says, "This is," the only true Christian response is, "Amen, so it is."

The devil's temptation of Christ to turn stones into bread after His fast was briefly mentioned before – how was it that Jesus rebuked him? (Mt 4:3-4) "One does not live by bread alone, but by every word that comes forth from the mouth of God," a quote from Deuteronomy 8:3:

"He therefore let you be afflicted with hunger, and then fed you with manna, a food unknown to you or your fathers, in order to show you that not by bread alone does man live, but by every word that comes forth from the mouth of God."

Recall that Jesus told the crowd that He was the bread come down from heaven, and added that though their fathers ate manna in the desert, they still died (John 6:49). Those who ate of the bread Jesus was to provide, would not die, but have life.

The passage with which Jesus rebuked the devil prefigured the new "bread of life," – for the Word of God did not only become man, He became the Bread of Life, which we need to have His life within us. (John 6:56)

Recommended Resources

The following are excellent sources for enriching your understanding of the Catholic Church's teachings and beliefs, as well as arguments and information to defend the Church in religious discussions.

Catechism of the Catholic Church (United States Catholic Conference, 1994)
Very simply, what Catholics believe. Very useful when the Church teaching is misrepresented, as it is the authoritative work on Church teachings.

Chesterton, G.K. ***Orthodoxy:The Romance of Faith*** (Various Publishers, 1908)
While not an apologetics book, Orthodoxy is a defense of the Catholic Church as a whole, written before the author became Catholic himself.

Hahn, Scott ***Catholic for a Reason: Scripture and the Mystery of the Family of God*** (Emmaus Road Publishing, Inc. 1998)

Hahn, Scott and Kimberly ***Rome Sweet Home: Our Journey to Catholicism*** (Ignatius Press, 1994)
Now a well-known Catholic theologian and apologist, Scott Hahn and his wife, Kimberly share the story of their conversion. There are a multitude of books by these authors, but the two listed here are more general. It is well worth it to look for a book by Scott or Kimberly on a specific aspect of the Faith that you are having difficulty explaining.

Keating, Karl ***Catholicism and Fundamentalism: The Attack on "Romanism" by "Bible Christians"***(Ignatius Press, 1988)
A very useful resource for defending the Faith, going even beyond the Bible and citing language differences and Church history. Addresses many common questions about the Catholic Church.

Keating, Karl ***What Catholics Really Believe – Setting the Record Straight*** (Servant Publications, 1992)
Answers to 52 common misconceptions about the Catholic Church.

Kellmeyer, Steven ***Bible Basics*** (Basilica Press, 2000)
A complete reference on Biblical foundations for six dozen Catholic doctrines. *Bible Basics* is an updated revision of Kellmeyer's *Scriptural Catholicism*.

Madrid, Patrick (ed) ***Surprised by Truth: 11 Converts give the Biblical and Historical Reasons for Becoming Catholic*** (Basilica Press, 1994)
Eleven testimonies from actual converts. Useful in two ways – first, the reasons they give are reasons that actually brought them to Catholicism, and second, by understanding their spiritual journeys you can hope to understand those of Protestants you know. Madrid has also edited other volumes in the series, with additional testimonies.

NOTES

The art of apologetics requires a persistent willingness to learn and grow. Use the following pages to write down questions for which you need to look up answers , Bible passages, or other pieces of information helpful for explaining your faith.

_____

_____

_____

_____

_____

_____

_____

_____

_____

_____

_____

_____

_____

_____

_____

_____

_____

_____

_____

NOTES

NOTES

NOTES

NOTES

NOTES

NOTES

NOTES

NOTES

NOTES

You may also be interested in:

GUERRILLA APOLOGETICS

PRO-LIFE
Guide

The Guerrilla Apologetics method, applied to life issues – so that you can be prepared to make convincing arguments to support the protection of human life in all its forms.

Guerrilla Apologetics
To order more copies of this book, or for information about other products, visit **www.GApologetics.com** or write:

Paul Nowak
PO Box 401
Mt. Laurel, NJ 08054

Printed in the United States
44481LVS00001B/47